Living with the Mind of Christ

Living *with the* Mind *of* Christ

A *Lenten Study for Adults*

JAMES A. HARNISH

ABINGDON PRESS / Nashville

LIVING WITH THE MIND OF CHRIST
A LENTEN STUDY FOR ADULTS

Copyright © 2005 by Abingdon Press

This book is printed on acid-free paper.

Library of Congress Catalog-in-Publication Data

Harnish, James A.
  Living with the mind of Christ : a Lenten study for adults / James A. Harnish.
    p. cm.
  ISBN 0-687-49651-9 (binding: pbk.; saddle stitched : alk. paper)
  1. Lent—Prayer-books and devotions—English. 2. Bible. N.T. Philippians II, 1-11—Criticism, interpretation, etc. 3. Bible. N.T. Luke—Criticism, interpretation, etc. I. Title.

  BV85.H347 2005
  242'.34—dc 22

                                                              2005024208

05 06 07 08 09 10 11 12 13 14— 10 9 8 7 6 5 4 3 2 1
MANUFACTURED IN THE UNITED STATES OF AMERICA

With gratitude for Peter and Elizabeth Storey,
courageous disciples who live
with the mind of Christ

Contents

Introduction

What does it take to change your mind? I'm not talking about changing your mind on little things: the model of your car, the destination for your next vacation, or the arrangement of the furniture in your living room. I'm talking about real change, radical change, fundamental change in the way we think, which results in practical changes in the way we live.

The biblical basis for our Lenten journey this season is one of the most eloquent passages in the entire New Testament, written by the apostle Paul and recorded in Philippians 2:1-11. Paul's purpose is as challenging as it is clear. He is out to change our minds. He called the Christians in Philippi to "be of the same mind, having the same love, being in full accord and of one mind" (v. 2). Paul challenges us, as he challenged them, to "let the same mind be in you that was in Christ Jesus" (v. 5).

The Greek word that is translated in English as "mind" describes a way of thinking that determines action. We might use the word *mind-set*. This refers to the fundamental foundation upon which we build our lives, the internal frame of reference through which we perceive everything else. It's the hard drive of our internal computer that directs all of our actions.

Make no mistake about it: The Christian faith is not about making minor adjustments on the exterior of our lives. The gospel is not a self-help manual to make life go a little smoother. The apostle is not a pop psychologist offering quick tips on self-improvement. Becoming a follower of Jesus requires a radical reorientation of our thinking that results in an equally radical transformation of our living. It calls for nothing less than a mental transplant, in which the mind-set with which Jesus came into this world, lived, died, and rose again becomes the mind-set by which we live, with which we die, and through which we are raised to new life. And that's a tall order indeed!

The traditional liturgy for Ash Wednesday invites us to "the observance of a holy Lent, by self-examination and repentance; by prayer, fasting, and self-denial; and by reading and meditating on God's holy Word" (*Book of Common Prayer* [New York: Seabury Press, 1979], 265). Like the forty days Jesus spent in the wilderness, these forty days (from Ash Wednesday to Easter, excluding Sundays) are the opportunity many of us need in order to wrestle with the deep issues of our lives and to discover new ways in which we can begin to live with the mind-set of Christ.

Love: The Power to Change Your Mind

Luke 10:25-37; Philippians 2:1-11

What does it take to change your mind?

One of my favorite movies is *Mr. Holland's Opus*, in which Richard Dreyfuss portrays a creatively frustrated, poorly paid, often misunderstood public high-school music teacher. A subplot in the movie is the story of a student who is line for a scholarship as a college wrestler but needs one more credit to graduate. The coach convinces Mr. Holland to take him into the band. With no musical background, the only instrument that seems like a possibility for this student is the bass drum. Unfortunately, he has absolutely no sense of rhythm. Mr. Holland works relentlessly to help this rhythmically challenged senior feel, hear, or see the beat of the music. He tries counting it out. He taps the student's feet with his own. He puts a football helmet on the guy's head and tries beating the rhythm into his brain.

Finally, we see Mr. Holland directing the band in John Philip Sousa's "Stars and Stripes Forever." He stops the band midway through the piece, just the way he has done every time the would-be drummer has missed the beat. Mr. Holland looks up to the drummer and says, "Congratulations. You've found the beat!" The entire band breaks into applause.

So, what would it take for us to begin to live by the rhythm of the mind-set of Christ? What does it take to change our minds?

Some people attempt to change our minds by force. Some try to convince us with logic or to manipulate us with advertising. But the apostle Paul was convinced that the one thing that really has the power to change our minds is love. For him, "being of the same mind" means "having the same love."

We've all seen this kind of change on a human level. We've known the stereotypical confirmed bachelor: good education, successful career, positive values, his mind set on never being tied down. Then some enchanted evening he sees her across a crowded room, and a mysterious power begins to change his mind. One day they stand at the altar, drawn together by an always amazing power that we call love.

Award-winning author Philip Yancey was one of those persons. He described his adolescent efforts at "erecting a strong stone fortress against love" because he thought himself unlovable. But one day during college, he met Janice. Yancey wrote, "Eventually the most powerful force in the universe, love, won out." His mind began to change. He wrote, "Hope aroused. I wanted to conquer worlds and lay them at her feet." For her birthday, Yancey learned Beethoven's *Sonata Pathétique* and invited her to hear him play it on the piano. "It was an offering to new life, and to her who had called it forth" (Philip Yancey, *Soul Survivor* [New York: Doubleday, 2001], 47-48). Yancey's mind-set, the fundamental perspective through which he viewed reality, began to change because he experienced the awesome power of human love. Janice's love brought out a whole new way of life in him.

That's a good place to begin, but the apostle Paul went far beyond mere human love. He coined a new word to describe it. The Greek word *agape* describes the unique love that transforms our minds into the mind of Christ.

The Love That Has the Power to Change Our Minds Is Defined by the Life, Death, and Resurrection of Jesus

New Testament scholars tell us that in the second chapter of Philippians, Paul picked up a creed or hymn that was used in worship in the early church to define the mind-set of Jesus Christ. Like

Mr. Holland trying to get the beat of the drum into the mind of his student, Paul is trying to get the rhythm of the way and will of the self-emptying love of God in Jesus into our brains, until we start to think, act, and live in rhythm with the heartbeat of God's love in Jesus Christ.

Across these weeks in Lent we will listen to that hymn and allow the rhythm of God's love in Christ to become the rhythm by which we live. At the outset, it is critically important for us to realize that when we use the word *love*, we are defining that term by nothing less than the self-giving love of God revealed in the life, death, and resurrection of Jesus Christ.

The Love That Has the Power to Change Our Minds Is Discovered in Community

One of the limitations of English pronouns is that the word *you* looks and sounds the same whether it's singular or plural. The exception, of course, is in the South, where the language has been improved by the use of "y'all" (for "you-all"). In Philippians 2, Paul is not writing to isolated individuals, but to the gathered community. He is saying, *"Y'all* be of the same mind. *Y'all* share the same love. *Y'all* be of one accord and of one mind. *Y'all* have among yourselves the same mind that was in Christ Jesus." The practical effect of the plural pronoun is that *agape* is best experienced in community with other disciples of Jesus Christ.

Lest we begin to think that the love of Christ is narrowly contained within the community of the church, however, it's important to remember that the "y'all" of God's love reaches out to the whole beloved human family.

Martin Luther King, Jr., declared that *agape* love was at the center of the Civil Rights movement. He called it "understanding, creative, redemptive good will for all [people] . . . the love of God working in the minds of men" (Martin Luther King Jr., *A Testament of Hope*, ed. James M. Washington [San Francisco: HarperSanFrancisco, 1986], 13).

Luther D. Ivory wrote that the "organizing principle"—we might say the "mind-set"—at the center of Dr. King's witness was "his faith in the radically involved, loving, and redeeming God of history." He believed that "radical agape love in action" is "God's ultimate will for humanity" and that "God's primary concern with human history was the restoration of the beloved human community." Ivory wrote:

> King understood God as radical agape love in action seeking to create, redeem, sustain, and restore community. Even when purposive human action tries to destroy it, God insists on community, and demonstrated (through the cross of Christ), that no sacrifice was too great to effect its restoration. (Luther D. Ivory, *Toward a Theology of Radical Involvement* [Nashville: Abingdon Press, 1997], 139)

The love that meets us at the cross is the sacrificial love of God for the whole human family.

The Love That Has the Power to Change Our Minds Takes Action in Human Relationships

The gospel message in Luke 10:25-37 contains one of Jesus' best-known stories. In response to the call to love God with his heart, soul, strength, and mind and to love his neighbor as he loved himself, a lawyer asked Jesus, "Who is my neighbor?"

In response to his question, Jesus told the story of the man who, going down from Jerusalem to Jericho, "fell into the hands of robbers, who stripped him, beat him, and went away, leaving him half dead." A priest and a Levite—good, upstanding, honorable, religious folk—passed by on the other side of the road. But a Samaritan—an ethnic outsider in a segregated society—saw the beaten man. Jesus used a very strong verb to say that the Samaritan "was moved with pity." The Samaritan picked the man up, bandaged his wounds, brought him to the inn, took care of him overnight, and left his credit card, so to speak, to pay for whatever the man needed.

Then Jesus turned the lawyer's question inside out by asking, "Which of these three, do you think, was a neighbor to the man who fell into the hands of the robbers?" The lawyer replied, "The one who showed him mercy." Jesus said, "You got that right. Go and do likewise" (Luke 10:37, paraphrased).

The parable of the good Samaritan is a dramatic description of the difference between the mind-set of the priest and the Levite, who saw the man in the road but walked by on the other side, and the mind-set of the Samaritan, who was so deeply moved with compassion that

14

he took action and made the other man's suffering his own. It's the difference between the mind-set of the person who asks, "Who is my neighbor?" and the person who asks, "Who acted as a neighbor to the other man?" It's a story about the way the love of God in Christ can change our minds.

She's gone to heaven, now, but I will never forget an eighty-something-year-old woman who had been raised on the white side of the segregated South. All of the changes of the 1960s had never changed her mind. She was a deeply committed Christian who attempted to relate to people in the love of Christ, but her basic mind-set about race was still stuck somewhere in the 1950s. One fall she signed up to participate in a DISCIPLE Bible study class. When she came to the first session, she was surprised to find an African American woman seated across the table. Over the next thirty-four weeks, as they wrestled together with the Scripture, that woman's mind-set about African American people was radically changed. When the older woman died, the African American woman was one of the persons who spoke as a witness to her life in the memorial service. She expressed her gratitude for the friendship they had shared and smiled with joy about the change that had come in the mind-set of her friend.

Love—the love of God in Christ—is like that; it has the power to change our minds.

Questions for Discussion and Reflection

1. What does it take to change your mind? Describe at least one significant change of mind that has come in your life. How did it happen? What was the result?

2. How have you experienced human love in ways that have changed your thinking or behavior?

3. When, where, or with whom have you experienced the love of Christ in Christian community? What difference does it make in your understanding of the faith for you to be in community with others?

4. How does your understanding of the love of Christ change your thinking about the "beloved community" of the human family? Read again Luther D. Ivory's description of agape. Where have you seen that sort of love at work?

5. Reread the story of the good Samaritan in Luke 10:25-37. Where would you find yourself in this story? In other words, with

which character in the story do you most identify at this moment in your life, and why?

6. What changes do you expect from this Lenten journey?

Prayer

Almighty and everlasting God, you hate nothing you have made and forgive the sins of all who are penitent: Create and make in us new and contrite hearts, that we, worthily lamenting our sins and acknowledging our wretchedness, may obtain of you, the God of all mercy, perfect remission and forgiveness; through Jesus Christ our Lord. Amen (*Book of Common Prayer* [New York: Seabury Press, 1979], 217).

Focus for the Week

The love of God revealed in Jesus Christ, discovered in community, and experienced in human relationships has the power to change our minds.

Servanthood: Breaking the Me-first Mind-set

Luke 22:14-27; Romans 8:5-6; Philippians 2:1-11

Through these weeks of Lent, we are focusing our attention on the challenge the apostle Paul places before us to live with the mind of Christ. The Christian life is not about a simple rearrangement of the external "stuff" in our lives. It is about a radical reorientation of the way we think that results in a radical change in the way we live. The gospel calls for a transformation so profound that Paul compares it to a mental transplant in which the same mind-set with which Jesus came, lived, died, and rose again becomes the mind-set in which we live, die, and are raised to new life. This week we focus our attention on Paul's description of Christ as the one who "emptied himself, / taking the form of a servant" (Philippians 2:7 RSV). Paul outlines the practical implications of that affirmation when he calls us to "do nothing from selfish ambition or conceit, but in humility regard others as better than yourselves" (Philippians 2:3). Living with the mind-set of Jesus means living with the mind-set of a servant.

The Greek word that Paul used for "mind" or "mind-set" in Philippians 2 is from the same root word he used in his letter to the Romans when he said that there are basically two kinds of people in this world. First, Paul said, there are people who "set their minds on the things of the flesh" (Romans 8:5). That's not necessarily a bad thing; it's just the ordinary thing. It's the ordinary mind-set of ordinary people who live their ordinary lives in the ordinary way of the ordinary world. It's a mind-set that begins with the assumption that I am the most important person in the world and that everything else is measured by how it fulfills what I need or want with little or no regard for anyone else.

By contrast, there are people who "set their minds" on the things of the Spirit. They are extraordinary people who live extraordinary lives because they focus their attention on the extraordinary way in which Jesus lived his life among us as one who serves (see Romans 8:5-6).

There is no better picture of the servant mind-set of Jesus than the story of the last Passover meal that Jesus shared with his followers. He broke the bread and said, "This is my body broken for you." He lifted the cup and said, "This is my blood shed for you." One person who saw Mel Gibson's movie *The Passion of the Christ* told me that the moment that touched her the most deeply was the flashback to the Last Supper during the very graphic portrayal of the Crucifixion. Hearing Jesus' words at the Last Supper in the context of what she was seeing on the screen in the suffering and sacrifice of the Crucifixion made this woman say that she would never take the bread and cup the same way again.

And what were the disciples doing during the Last Supper? Luke records that "a dispute also arose among them as to which one of them was to be regarded as the greatest" (Luke 22:24). Jesus was on his way to the cross, and his disciples were bickering about which of them was the greatest. Jesus was preparing to die, and they were fussing about who would get the best seats at the table.

Jesus acknowledged that their dispute was typical of the ordinary world where the ordinary mind-set is focused on self-interest, a world where people with wealth, position, and power lord it over others and push other people around. But, Jesus said, that's not the way it will be for his disciples. The mind-set of his followers will not be the mind-set of one who is here to be served but the mind-set of one who is here to serve.

We might as well face it: We all are afflicted by the "me-first mind-set." It's a radical self-orientation that causes us to assume that we are here to get what we want, when we want it, the way we want it and that everyone and everything else exists to serve our interests. Thomas Long, a professor at the Candler School of Theology at

Emory University, diagnosed this cultural ailment by saying that "something of a perfect storm of self-absorption has formed, born of the low-pressure front of basic selfishness, merged with a wave of narcissistic preoccupation with the individual as the arbiter of all moral judgments and the tidal surge of lust for material possessions" (Michael A. Turner and William F. Malambri III, eds., *A Peculiar Prophet* [Nashville: Abingdon Press, 2004], 85).

I recently shared with my congregation a "top ten" list to complete the sentence "You might have a 'me-first mind-set' if . . ."

10. you pulled into a parking space ahead of the retired guy in the white Buick with the Michigan license place who had been waiting with his turn signal flashing while the other car pulled out;

9. you sneaked into the express checkout lane in a crowded grocery store with more than ten items;

8. you emptied the last scoop of ice cream, finished the last piece of pecan pie, or sneaked away with the last chocolate chip cookie in the jar when nobody else in the family was looking;

7. you forgot to tell your parents about the call that came in on "call waiting" while you were talking to your friend;

6. you passed along that dirty little rumor about a friend because it somehow made you look better;

5. you voted for a candidate solely on the basis of what would benefit your bottom line with no regard for what might benefit people who have less than you do;

4. you accepted credit from your boss for a job you knew someone else had done;

3. you assume that anyone who doesn't like the same movies, music, or TV shows that you do is clearly a person with little or no taste;

2. you gave your spouse a birthday gift that was something you really wanted for yourself;

1. you feel a sigh of relief in knowing that you aren't as poorly dressed, ill-mannered, unimportant, unintelligent, or just plain tacky as all the self-centered sinners who are sitting around you in the congregation.

We are all afflicted with the "me-first mind-set." The only way I know to be set free from its bondage is to begin to discover the mind-set of Jesus, who came among us not to be served, but to serve. In order to see what this mind-set looks like, let's rivet our attention on two things that Paul said about Jesus in the sixth and seventh verses of Philippians 2.

First, Paul declared that Christ was "in the form of God" (v. 6). The Greek word Paul used here is *morphe,* which describes the essential character or nature of a thing. People who understand video technology know what "morphing" is. It's the way a computer merges one image into another. We could say that the essential character of the infinite God was "morphed" into Jesus. In Jesus, we see the core identity of the infinite God in human form.

The second thing Paul said about Jesus is that "*though* he was in the form of God," he "emptied himself" (vv. 6 and 7, emphasis added). An alternate translation might instead say of Jesus that it was "*because* he was in the form of God [that] he emptied himself." *Because* Jesus was the human expression of the infinite God, *because* Jesus did not see being equal with God as some sort of power trip to be grasped or exploited, he chose to serve rather than to be served. *Because* he was the living expression of the self-giving love of God, he took the form of a servant. Jesus' life as a servant was not just something he did; it is basic to his identity as the one who is the *morphe*—the likeness—of God.

When Jesus healed a man who was blind and poor, provided food to hungry people, took children in his arms, touched a person suffering from leprosy, wept beside his friend's grave, forgave a woman who had committed adultery, redirected the life of a greedy tax collector, and took a basin and towel and got down on his knees to wash his disciples' feet, he was not performing some kind of temporary masquerade or playing a temporary role. Rather, he was demonstrating for us in human terms the love that is in the heart of God.

When Jesus surrendered himself in vulnerable weakness to all of the evil power of the world and died, naked and bleeding on the cross, it was not a disguise of who God is; it was the revelation of who God is. And when God raised Jesus from the tomb, it was not as if Jesus was lifted up to some ethereal cloud where he could sit around on a golden throne and be pampered and powerful. When God raised Jesus from death, God was saying that the life we have seen in Jesus is the life that God intends for the whole creation. In Philippians 2:9-11, Paul said, "Therefore," because Jesus chose to be a servant, "God also highly exalted him / and gave him the name / that is above every name, / so that at the name of Jesus / every knee should bend, / in heaven and on earth and under the earth, / and every tongue should confess / that Jesus Christ is Lord." Ultimately, the whole created order will fall on its knees before the self-giving, self-sacrificing, servant-hearted love revealed in Christ.

Servanthood is not just what Jesus did; it's who Jesus is as the One who is in the image and likeness of God.

Albert Schweitzer, who modeled Christian servanthood for an entire generation, once said, "I don't know what your destiny will be but one thing I know, the only ones among you who will be really happy are those who have sought and found how to serve" (Dan Wakefield, *Returning*, [New York: Doubleday, 1988] page 201). The apostle Paul might just as well have said that, too.

Questions for Discussion and Reflection

1. What image comes to your mind when you hear the word *servant*? Explain your answer in some detail, including reasons why the word *servant* brings to mind for you the image(s) it does.

2. Read Romans 8:5-6. What is your understanding of the contrasting mind-sets Paul describes there?

3. How can you identify with the disciples at the Passover supper (see Luke 22:14-27)? Where have you seen a dispute about who is the greatest?

4. How have you experienced the "me-first mind-set" in the culture around us? How have you experienced it in your own life?

5. What difference does it make for you to hear that it is *because* Jesus was in the form of God that he became a servant? How does this description influence your understanding of the nature of God?

6. What specific steps can you take to live with the mind-set of a servant?

Prayer

He deigns in flesh to appear,
Widest extremes to join;
To bring our vileness near,
And make us all divine:
And we the life of God shall know,
For God is manifest below.

(*John and Charles Wesley: Selected Prayers, Hymns, Journal Notes, Sermons, Letters and Treatises,* Frank Waling, ed. [New York: Paulist Press, 1981], 282)

Focus for the Week

Giving himself as a servant to others is not just what Jesus did; it defines who Jesus was and who Jesus calls us to be.

Faithful Suffering: The Foolishness of the Cross

1 Corinthians 1:18-31; Philippians 1:27-30

A friend of mine was leaving the theater after seeing the movie *The Passion of the Christ,* when he noticed a man in tears, standing on the sidewalk, saying to no one in particular and to everyone in general, "Jesus suffered, so I don't have to."

Hearing those words, my friend's mind moved to the book of Acts, where the Lord called a Christ follower named Ananias to find Saul, who had just experienced his conversion along the Damascus Road. Ananias had heard about Saul. He knew that Saul was committed to nothing less than a full-scale program of terrorism to destroy the early Christian movement. Ananias had good reason to question whether finding Saul was such a great idea, but the Lord wouldn't let him off the hook. The Lord told Ananias to go to Saul, "for he is an instrument whom I have chosen to bring my name before Gentiles and kings and before the people of Israel; I myself will show him how much he must suffer for the sake of my name" (Acts 9:15-16). Against what I am sure was his better human judgment, Ananias found Saul, tutored him in the early stages of his conversion, and all the rest, as they say, is history.

Without depreciating the sincerity of a stranger's response to the movie, it struck my friend that Paul never would have said, "Jesus suffered, so I don't have to." Quite the opposite. From the earliest days of his life with Christ, Paul knew that following God's call would mean personal identification with the suffering of his Lord. In one of the most autobiographical passages he ever wrote, Paul defined the mind-set that directed his behavior:

> I want to know Christ and the power of his resurrection and the sharing of his sufferings by becoming like him in his death, if somehow I may attain the resurrection from the dead. (Philippians 3:10-11)

My guess is that *suffering* isn't exactly what we thought we were signing on for when we started coming to church. If you listen carefully to a lot of what passes for evangelistic preaching these days, you'll hear a message that is ultimately about "me": satisfying *my* needs, protecting *my* lifestyle, securing *my* nation, ensuring both *my* temporal and eternal happiness. Used this way, the gospel becomes a self-help program for everything from getting rid of excess weight to getting rich on the stock market.

Throughout the Gospels, however, the call of Jesus is a clear contradiction of that kind of self-protective mind-set. With relentless consistency, Jesus said:

> Was it not necessary that the Messiah should suffer these things and then enter into his glory? (Luke 24:26)

> Whoever does not carry the cross and follow me cannot be my disciple. (Luke 14:27)

> If any want to become my followers, let them deny themselves and take up their cross and follow me. For those who want to save their life will lose it, and those who lose their life for my sake, and for the sake of the gospel, will save it. (Mark 8:34-35)

Paul's words in the second chapter of his letter to the Philippians (which we examined in the first and second weeks of this study) build on his words at the end of chapter 1: "[God] has graciously granted you the privilege not only of believing in Christ, but of suffering for him as well—since you are having the same struggle that you saw I had and now hear that I still have" (Philippians 1:29-30). To live with the mind-set of Christ means following Jesus in the way that leads to the cross. We are given the *privilege* of sharing in the suffering love of Christ for this world.

During a sabbatical with the Methodists in South Africa, I was reminded of one of the most important lessons they have to teach us, namely, that we will know the love of God that sent Jesus to suffer on the cross, not when we escape suffering, but when we embrace the suffering of others. In his book *With God in the Crucible*, former South African Methodist bishop Peter Storey challenges every form of comfortable discipleship. Out of his experience in the struggle against apartheid, he writes, "There is power in faithful suffering! Where most religions offer escape from suffering and increases in comfort, the Christian faith makes this astounding claim. . . . If you want to know whether God is alive, you must go, not to where all is well, but into places of brokenness and suffering. . . . There are depths of reality, dimensions of God, releases of healing energy, that flow into this world only through the power of faithful suffering" (Peter Storey, *With God in the Crucible* [Nashville: Abingdon Press, 2002], 80-81).

To the world, of course, talk of suffering sounds like utter foolishness or, even worse, like the ultimate expression of neurotic self-absorption. Paul acknowledged as much in his letter to Corinth when he called the message of the cross "foolishness to those who are perishing, but to us who are being saved it is the power of God." At the same time, he declared that "God's foolishness is wiser than human wisdom, and God's weakness is stronger than human strength. . . . God chose what is foolish in the world to shame the wise; God chose what is weak in the world to shame the strong; God chose what is low and despised in the world, things that are not, to reduce to nothing things that are" (1 Corinthians 1:18, 25, 27-28).

The way of suffering love looks downright foolish to the world. So foolish that some Christians try to reshape Jesus into their own image.

The headline in the *New York Times* read, "The Return of the Warrior Jesus." The article began with Tim LaHaye and Jerry Jenkins's description of the final coming of Christ in the last volume of their Left Behind series. The *Times* wrote, "Few have portrayed [Christ] wreaking more carnage on the unbelieving world. . . . With all the gruesome detail of a Hollywood horror movie, Jesus eviscerates the flesh of millions of unbelievers merely by speaking" (David D. Kirkpatrick, "The Warrior Jesus" *New York Times* April 4, 2004).

The article described a cultural shift from "the gentle, pacifist Jesus of the Crucifixion" to "a more muscular warrior Jesus of the Second Coming, the Lamb is making way for the Lion." The writer saw the same shift in Mel Gibson's version of the passion. "When you see [Jesus] stand up at the end of the movie, he reminds you of Schwarzenegger."

Gibson's Jesus didn't look like Arnold Schwarzenegger to me, but the reviewer in the *Christian Century* magazine raised the same concern. "The Christ in this movie doesn't represent anything Christlike. . . . Instead, he is a victim with the guts to stand up after a beating. . . . To reduce Jesus Christ to a tough dude who can take a licking and keep on ticking is not exactly a feat that calls for hosannas" (John Petrakis, "Tough Guy" *Christian Century*, March 23, 2004).

As appealing as macho images of Jesus may be, they prey on my imagination as we make our journey toward Holy Week. The closer we get to the cross, the more they disturb me. The *Times* writer assumed that we have to choose either "the effeminate . . . marshmallowy, Santa Claus Jesus" or "a darker, more martial, macho concept of the Messiah." My problem is that I can't make either of those descriptions fit with scripture. Neither represents the central core of Christian teaching, and neither of them describes the way I have come to know and experience the presence of Christ.

When we break the bread and lift the cup over the Lord's Table, we remember the One who was equal with God but who did not see equality with God as something to be held tightly. He is the one who emptied himself, literally "poured himself out," for us in the ultimate act of nonviolent, self-giving love. When we extinguish the Tenebrae candles and leave the church in darkness on Good Friday, we enter the darkness with the One who humbled himself, came among us as a servant, and was obedient to death—even death on the cross. There's nothing about the story that is either "marshmallowy" or "macho." The way Jesus lived and died breaks our cultural molds as it demonstrates the difference between the divine strength of powerless love and the human weakness of loveless power.

And on Easter morning, we will celebrate the great "therefore" of the resurrection. "Therefore God also highly exalted him / and gave him the name / that is above every name" (Philippians 2:9). Notice that Paul said "therefore," not "in spite of this." The resurrection does not contradict the way of nonviolent, suffering, self-giving love; it confirms that the way Jesus went to the cross is the way God intends to save this whole lost and broken creation. Even in the Revelation, the central figure is not the "macho Jesus" of fiction, but "the Lamb that was slain" (Revelation 13:8 RSV). The Christ who comes in glory is the same Jesus who died for us on the cross. We do not need, and we are not given, a macho Jesus. We desperately need, and we are graciously given, the One who died and rose again.

The shocking thing about the gospel is that Jesus actually expects us to take up the cross of nonviolent, suffering love and follow him. Jesus didn't attract fans; he called disciples. He didn't give us what we want; he revealed what we most deeply need. The New Testament expects every disciple of Jesus to actually become like Christ, not in the details of crucifixion, but in the mind-set that Jesus demonstrated in the way he went to the cross. The point of the story is not just to be impressed with Jesus' suffering but to share in his suffering for others; not just to know that he died for us but to discover what it will mean for us to die to the controlling power of our own self-interest and take up the interest of the world he came to save.

Questions for Discussion and Reflection

1. Have you seen the movie *The Passion of the Christ*? If so, how did it affect you? What other powerful or compelling portrayals of Christ have you witnessed or experienced, and in what ways were you moved or affected?

2. Reread Philippians 1:27-30. How do you feel when you read the apostle Paul's words about sharing the suffering of Christ? What do you think he meant by these remarks? How could it be a "privilege" to share in suffering?

3. How have you seen or experienced what Peter Storey called "faithful suffering"? Where have you seen the presence of God in places of brokenness and suffering?

4. What is your reaction to the idea of a "warrior Jesus"?

5. How have you experienced the "foolishness of the cross" (see 1 Corinthians 1:18-29)?

6. How would you describe what it means to follow Christ in the way of "nonviolent, suffering, self-giving love"? In whose life have you seen that mind-set at work?

Prayer

Almighty and everliving God, in your tender love for the human race you sent your Son our Savior Jesus Christ to take upon him our nature, and to suffer death upon the cross, giving us the example of his great humility: Mercifully grant that we may walk in the way of his suffering, and also share in his resurrection. Amen (*Book of Common Prayer* [New York: Seabury Press, 1979], 219).

Focus for the Week

To live with the mind-set of Christ means following Jesus in the way that leads to the cross. We are given the *privilege* of sharing in the suffering love of Christ for this world.

Surrender: The Moment of Letting Go

Luke 9:18-27; Philippians 2:1-11; 3:4b-14

To celebrate my birthday, my wife took me to see *Cirque du Soleil*. It's an absolutely astonishing performance of tumblers, acrobats, and dancers. I have to admit that the contortionist who twisted herself inside out so that I couldn't tell whether she was coming or going was a little weird to me, but the rest were just amazing. The finale was a team of trapeze artists, soaring back and forth high above the gasping crowd. They flew through the air as if they had been born with wings.

Watching them, my memory carried me back to my stage debut in the third grade. The theme of the end-of-the-year musical program was "The Circus," and our class was assigned that old song that goes, "He flies through the air with the greatest of ease, / the daring young man on the flying trapeze."

For some oddball reason, I was chosen to be the man on the flying trapeze! I guess they wanted the skinniest kid in the class. I remember a tank top with sequins that must have hung like an old pillowcase over my formless body. And I remember the little girl who was my partner. With no trapeze, we just stumbled across the stage while the rest of the kids sang the song. The best thing about that story is that my parents did not own a video camera!

29

As I watched the real men on the flying trapeze, I realized that we were all waiting for one particular moment. It's that moment when the guy on one bar chooses to let go. He soars through the air in absolute trust that his partner will be coming from the other side to grasp him with his extended arms. The whole performance is focused on that moment of letting go.

We have a word for that moment of letting go in the life of Christian discipleship. The word is *surrender*. It's that moment in which a person chooses to let go of one thing in order to reach out in trust for another. It is the moment of letting go of something in ourselves in order to grasp a new life in Christ.

The process by which we discover the mind-set of Christ ultimately leads us to a place of surrender, that place in our spiritual journey where we let go of our old mind-set and reach out to grasp the new mind-set of Jesus Christ. It's all about surrender; it's about that moment of letting go.

We know what that surrender meant for Jesus. The apostle Paul described it in a powerful way in the hymn or affirmation of faith that he plucked out of the worship of the early church and pasted into his letter to the Philippians (2:5-11). Can you feel the movement in that text? It's like a trapeze bar that swings down into the depth of our humanity and then soars back up into the glory of God. It's the movement of the One who refuses to hold on to the divine prerogative but releases himself to come to be with us, all the way into our death. And in that self-emptying love, he is raised to new life in the resurrection.

That's what it meant for Jesus. And Jesus made it perfectly clear that that is precisely what he expects from his followers: "If any want to become my followers, let them deny themselves and take up their cross daily and follow me. For those who want to save their life will lose it, and those who lose their life for my sake will save it" (Luke 9:23-24).

Deny yourself? Well, if there is anything we don't want to do, that's it! We're into affirming ourselves, satisfying ourselves, celebrating ourselves, getting what we want. It has become the perverted expression of what we call "the American dream." But Paul challenges us to look not only to our own interests, but also to the interests of others. Jesus calls us to deny ourselves. Jesus challenges us to let go of the arrogant mind-set that measures everything in life by the way it serves our self-interest and to deny our desire to do it "my way" in order to do it "his way."

Deny yourself, Jesus said, and take up your cross daily. I'm glad Luke included that word *daily*. It says to me that the whole business of surrender, of releasing ourselves and letting go, is not a one-time occurrence but that it becomes the basic pattern, the fundamental mind-set by which we live. In the religious tradition in which I grew up, I kept looking for one dramatic spiritual experience that would set me up for the rest of my life. Every summer at youth camp and during the "altar call" at an old Methodist camp meeting, I would "go forward" in search of the one-time denial of self that would wipe away all of the internal struggles of my adolescent soul. But that's not how it is worked out, and that's not what the Bible says. Jesus calls us to take up our cross daily. In Christian discipleship, letting go of our own prerogatives, surrendering ourselves to Christ, becomes the ordinary pattern of our daily lives.

This kind of surrender is critically important because Jesus said that anyone who tries to save his life will lose it. If we try to grasp our life, hold it tightly in our fist, protect our own self-interest from the interests of others, it will shrivel up and die in the narrow confines of our self-absorption. The only way to find life is to release it, to let it go, to be set free by giving ourselves to something larger than our own self-interest. Then we will find life, Jesus said, and find it abundantly.

We know what this meant for Jesus. We know what Jesus said it would mean for his disciples. And we know what it meant for the apostle Paul. In the third chapter of his letter to the Philippians, Paul became very personal as he described what it meant for him to let go of his own prerogatives in order to claim his new life in Christ. He clicked off the list of all the things he had going for himself: position, power, status, education, probably wealth . . . in short, all of the things that the world grasps and holds so tightly. Then Paul declared:

> Yet whatever gains I had, these I have come to regard as loss because of Christ. More than that, I regard everything as loss because of the surpassing value of knowing Christ Jesus my Lord. For his sake I have suffered the loss of all things, and I regard them as rubbish, in order that I may gain Christ. (Philippians 3:7-10)

The apostle who lost everything that he thought was important to his identity then described the way the life of surrender became the daily pattern of his life.

> Not that I have already obtained this or have already reached the goal; but I press on to make it my own, because Christ Jesus has made me his own. Beloved, I do not consider that I have made it my own; but this one thing I do: forgetting what lies behind and straining forward to what lies ahead, I press on toward the goal for the prize of the heavenly call of God in Christ Jesus. (Philippians 3:12-14)

J. B. Phillips paraphrased Paul's words to say, "I keep going on, grasping ever more firmly that purpose for which Christ Jesus grasped me" (JBP). It is the continuing process of letting go in order to take hold of the new life Christ has for us.

We know what surrender looked like for Jesus. We know what it looked like for Paul. And we know what it looked like for a hobbit named Bilbo Baggins.

The fundamental theme of J. R. R. Tolkien's The Lord of the Rings trilogy is the way in which the power of evil takes possession of anyone who thinks they can possess it. The only way to be free from it is to let go. The moment comes when Bilbo has to decide whether he is willing to let the ring go.

> Gandalf looked again very hard at Bilbo, and there was a gleam in his eyes. "I think, Bilbo," he said quietly, "I should leave it behind. Don't you want to?"
>
> "Well yes—and no. Now it comes to it, I don't like parting with it at all, I may say. And I don't really see why I should. . . . It is mine, I tell you. My own. . . . And I shall keep it, I say."
>
> Gandalf stood up. He spoke sternly. "You will be a fool if you do, Bilbo," he said. "You make that clearer with every word you say. It has got far too much hold on you. Let it go! And then you can go yourself, and be free. . . . I am not trying to rob you, but to help you. I wish you would trust me, as you used."
>
> Bilbo stood for a moment tense and undecided. Presently he sighed. "All right," he said with an effort. "I will." Then he shrugged his shoulders, and smiled rather ruefully. . . . He drew a deep breath. "And now I really must be starting, or somebody else will catch me. . . . He picked up his bag and moved to the door.
>
> "You have still got the ring in your pocket," said [Gandalf].

Finally, Bilbo releases the ring and, as he walks away he says, "I am as happy now as I have ever been, and that is saying a great deal" (J. R. R. Tolkien, *Fellowship of the Ring* [New York: Random House, 1965], 59-62).

The gymnasts and acrobats in *Cirque du Soleil* have no expectation that I will come out of the audience and join them up there on the trapeze, but Jesus does expect us to join him. When Christ calls us to surrender, he is not trying to rob us, but to help us—indeed, to save us.

Questions for Reflection and Discussion

1. If time permits, read Paul's entire letter to the Philippians, chapters 1 through 4. (It will take about twelve minutes.) How does the letter as a whole inform your understanding of Philippians 2:1-11?

2. What does the word *surrender* mean to you? How does the image of the trapeze artists help you grasp the meaning of that term?

3. Reread Luke 9:23-24. How does Jesus' call in this passage speak to you? What would it mean for you to "deny yourself" and to "take up your cross daily" in order to follow Christ?

4. When have you faced a moment of "letting go" in your journey of faith? What were you called to release in order to take hold of new life in Christ?

5. In what ways can you identify with Paul's witness in Philippians 3:7-14?

6. What specific surrender are you called to make in your discipleship today?

Prayer

Were the whole realm of nature mine,
That were an offering far too small;
Love so amazing, so divine,
Demands my soul, my life, my all.

> (From "When I Survey the Wondrous Cross," words by Isaac Watts; 1707)

Focus for the Week

Living with the mind-set of Christ means letting go of ourselves to follow Jesus to the cross.

Humility: Moving Up by Coming Down

Luke 14:7-24; 18:9-14; Philippians 2:1-11

Henri Nouwen, the Catholic priest and author whose words continue to move so many people so deeply, touched upon the central core of the apostle Paul's words to the Philippians when he wrote, "Our lives in this technological and highly competitive society are characterized by a pervasive drive for upward mobility." Nouwen described the way our lives are structured around climbing to the top of whatever we define as the ladder of success. He wrote, "Our very sense of vitality is dependent upon being part of the upward pull and upon the joy provided by the rewards given on the way up."

The gospel, however, moves in precisely the opposite direction. Nouwen went on to say, "The story of our salvation stands radically over and against the philosophy of upward mobility. The great paradox which Scripture reveals to us is that real and total freedom can only be found through downward mobility. The Word of God came down to us and lived among us as a slave. The divine way is indeed the downward way" ("The Selfless Way of Christ," *Sojourners*, June 1981, 13-14).

The journey downward into the mind-set of Jesus brings us this week to the word *humility*, which is not exactly the most popular commodity in our world today. The apostle Paul calls us to have the same mind-set, the same attitude, the same way of thinking, acting, and living as Christ Jesus, who, he said, "humbled himself."

When our church's worship team began studying Philippians 2:1-11, one member of the team, who just happens to believe that anything that really matters in life has been expressed in a country song, immediately recited, "Lord, it's hard to be humble when you're perfect in every way." That's not far removed from Ted Turner's confession, "If I had a little more humility I would be perfect" (*New York Public Library Book of Twentieth-century American Quotations*, ed. Stephen Donadio et al. [New York: Warner Books, 1992], 272).

Archbishop Desmond Tutu said he learned a lesson in humility in an airplane when the flight attendant told him that a fellow passenger wanted him to autograph a book. Tutu said that he attempted to project appropriate modesty while thinking to himself that there were evidently people on the plane who recognized a good thing when they saw it. But then, as the attendant handed the book to him, she said, "You are Bishop Muzorewa, aren't you?" (Desmond Tutu, *God Has a Dream* [New York: Doubleday, 2004], 82).

Humility is the theme of the parable we study this week. Luke records, "On one occasion when Jesus was going to the house of a leader of the Pharisees to eat a meal on the sabbath, they were watching him closely" (Luke 14:1).

With much humility of my own, I dare to say that I know in some small way how it feels to be watched the way Jesus was watched. Some people look at me as if there were three sexes: men, women, and preachers. It happens when I offer the invocation at a civic or business event. The folk at the registration table give me a big name tag that says "The Reverend James A. Harnish." I start wandering around during the predinner reception, and when folk see the title on my name tag, they start acting as if I'm checking out what they have in their glass.

The next time that happens, I think I'll do what Jesus did. Jesus started watching *them*. Luke says that "he noticed how the guests chose the places of honor" (Luke 14:7). Jesus watched the way these guests were jockeying for the best seats at the table, and it gave him the material for a parable. It's a parable of contrasts, one of his "do this and don't do this" parables.

First, he said, don't be like the wedding guest who acted as if he were the guest of honor. He went straight to the head table and took the best seat in the house.

36

I've been seated at the head table. It feels good to be with the dignitaries, getting served first, looking down on all the others crowded around the tables on the floor. The problem, Jesus said, came when the dinner host said, "I'm sorry to tell you this, but the guest of honor has just arrived." Then, in disgrace, this guest who had assumed the seat of honor had to move down to the lowest place. Jesus told us not to be like that arrogant dinner guest. Instead, he gave these instructions for dinner table etiquette:

> Go and sit down at the lowest place, so that when your host comes, he may say to you, "Friend, move up higher"; then you will be honored in the presence of all who sit at the table with you. (Luke 14:10)

Jesus concluded his remarks by paraphrasing an Old Testament proverb: "For all who exalt themselves will be humbled, and those who humble themselves will be exalted" (Luke 14:11; see also Proverbs 29:23).

Look closely at the verbs in that proverb. Jesus said that all who *exalt* themselves (active voice) *will be humbled* (passive voice) and those who *humble* themselves (active voice) *will be exalted* (passive voice). In each case, the subject acts and then is acted upon. We choose our actions, but we do not choose the consequences of those actions. And Jesus said that the actions and the consequences move in precisely the opposite directions. Those who exalt themselves, who actively puff themselves up, will be humbled; but those who actively humble themselves will ultimately be exalted.

Jesus referred to the same proverb again in the story of two men who went up to the Temple to pray. One was a Pharisee, which meant that he was a law-abiding, rule-keeping, tithe-paying man. Standing, he looked up to heaven and told God how good he was. The other man was a tax collector, which meant that he was in cahoots with the occupational forces of the Roman Empire. He was a crook, a sinner. He would not even lift his head toward heaven but instead beat upon his chest and prayed, "God, be merciful to me, a sinner!" (Luke 18:13). And in concluding his telling of this story, Jesus repeated the proverb:

> I tell you, this man went down to his home justified rather than the other; for all who exalt themselves will be humbled, but all who humble themselves will be exalted. (Luke 18:14)

37

Most of us would probably confess that there is something about the word *humility* that turns us off. It is loaded down with all sorts of damaging images from the culture around us. But when the Bible talks about humility, it's not talking about being a doormat upon which everyone else wipes his or her dirty feet. When Jesus calls us to humble ourselves, he is not describing phony piety in which we pretend that we don't value our own life, talents, and gifts; he is not turning an inferiority complex into a virtue. When the apostle Paul challenges us to live with a mind-set of humility, he is not talking about some sort of neurotic self-hatred that keeps people as prisoners of abusive relationships. *Humility* is light years removed from *humiliation*.

But the challenge is still before us to have the same mind-set as Jesus, who humbled himself. So, let's look more closely at the "dos" and "don'ts" of living with a mind-set of humility.

First, *don't take yourself too seriously*. Don't overestimate your own importance. In his letter to Rome, Paul advised not to think of yourself more highly than you ought to think but to have a sober estimate of your own importance (Romans 12:3). We are all tempted to be like the rooster with the sore throat who was convinced that the sun wouldn't rise if he couldn't crow.

Writing in the *Christian Century* magazine, Ronald Goetz described healthy humility this way:

> The call for humility is a call for simple realism. . . . Humility is an honest and objective reflection of our real relationship to God. The fact is that we *are* all dependent. All that we have comes from God—our lives, our salvation, our hope, our Christ. God has given all; nothing is our own . . . [Humility] is a simple, objective recognition of the reality of God. ("Proud to Be Humble," *Christian Century*, February 28, 1979, 207)

Rick Warren, the author of *The Purpose-Driven Life*, has been recognized as one of the most influential writers in the country, and yet there is a quality of self-effacing humility about him. I heard him speak at a leadership event in which he said that one of the biggest problems for many of us is that we take ourselves too seriously and don't take God seriously enough. He pointed out that the words *humor* and *humility* come from the same root word, and he said that if we learn to laugh at ourselves, we will always have plenty of material!

G. K. Chesterton, the British novelist, editor, and theologian, pointed out that people who study the lives of mystical saints often describe their power of "levitation." Chesterton pushed the image to say that one of the characteristics of any saint is his or her power of "levity." Chesterton wrote, "One 'settles down' into a sort of selfish seriousness; but one has to rise to a gay self-forgetfulness. . . . It is easy to be heavy: hard to be light. Satan fell by force of gravity. . . . Angels can fly because they take themselves so lightly" (*Orthodoxy*, [Mineola, N.Y.: Dover, 2004], pages 120-21).

That's the "don't" instruction. But "do" *treat everyone else like royalty.* Treat every other person as if he or she were the guest of honor at your table. Jesus makes the point by giving some rather odd instructions for the invitation list for a dinner party:

> When you give a luncheon or a dinner, do not invite your friends or your brothers or your relatives or rich neighbors, in case they may invite you in return, and you would be repaid. But when you give a banquet, invite the poor, the crippled, the lame, and the blind. And you will be blessed, because they cannot repay you, for you will be repaid at the resurrection of the righteous. (Luke 14:12-14)

Jesus goes on to tell the story of a man who was going to throw a great banquet. He invited all of his friends, but they started making excuses and wouldn't come. So, he sent his servants out into the streets to pick up anybody they could find to come to dinner and to fill up the house (see Luke 14:15-24).

If God is the host in this parable, then there are only two options for us. We are either the snotty self-impressed guests who turned down the invitation, or we are the motley crew that the servants dragged in from the streets. We are either like the self-righteous Pharisee who patted himself on the back, or we are like the humble tax collector who knew he needed mercy. The point is that none of us swaggers into the kingdom of God. The only folk who show up around the banquet table are those who know they have no business being there. We are welcomed to the feast by an extravagantly generous host who brings us in, not because we are all that good, but because *God* is.

If that's the way God treats us, then we are called to treat everyone else the same way: like the guest of honor at the banquet. Paul describes our behavior this way:

Do nothing from selfish ambition or conceit, but in humility regard others as better than yourselves. Let each of you look not to your own interests, but to the interests of others. Let the same mind be in you that was in Christ Jesus, who . . . humbled himself. (Philippians 2:3-6, 8)

Think back across your life for a moment. Think about some of the really great people in your life. I'll bet they are the people who treated you like royalty, people who acted as if you were the most important person in the room, people who made you feel that you really mattered. The great people in our lives generally are not those who try to impress us with their greatness, but who release the greatness within us.

Exalt yourself, Jesus said, and you will be humbled. It takes only a tiny pin to puncture the egotistical fantasy of folk who blow themselves up larger than life. But humble yourself, have a sane sense of your own value, treat everyone like royalty, and you will be exalted. The only way to go up is by coming down, because, after all, that's just what Jesus did.

Questions for Discussion and Reflection

1. What does the word *humility* mean for you? What images or experiences come to your mind when you hear that word?

2. Look closely at Jesus' words in Luke 14:11. What does it mean for you to "exalt yourself" or to "humble yourself"? Have you ever had an experience similar to that of the dinner guest in Jesus' parable (see Luke 14:8-10)? If so, describe it.

3. Reread Luke 18:10-14. How can you identify with either or both of the two men who prayed at the Temple?

4. Who are the persons who have modeled Christlike humility for you? Who are the people who have treated you royally and have released greatness within you?

5. What changes would need to be made in your life in order for you to live with a mind-set of humility? What steps will you take to make these changes?

Prayer

Almighty and everliving God, in your tender love for the human race you sent your Son our Savior Jesus Christ to take upon him our nature, and to suffer death upon the cross, giving us the example of his great humility: Mercifully grant that we may walk in the way of his suffering, and also share in his resurrection; through Jesus Christ our Lord. Amen (*Book of Common Prayer* [New York: Seabury Press, 1979], 219).

Focus for the Week

Living with the mind-set of humility means being a gracious guest at the table and welcoming others there, too.

Obedience: How Far Will You Go?

Luke 22:39-46; John 1:1-3, 14; Philippians 2:1-11

One of the most popular dive spots along the eastern coast of Florida is in John Pennekamp Coral Reef State Park in the Florida Keys. Even novice divers can descend to see a nine-foot statute of Christ that rests on the ocean floor. It's called the *Christ of the Deep*. In addition to being one of the most photographed dive sites in the world, it's also a popular site for underwater marriages, but I'm grateful no one has ever asked me to perform one!

The bronze figure was cast from the same mold as the figure that stands in the Mediterranean Sea at San Fruttosa Bay, near Genoa, Italy, where it is known as *Il Christo Degli Abissi*, the *Christ of the Abyss*. The hands of Christ are raised above his head. He is looking up toward the sunlit surface of the ocean. Some divers see it as a posture of praise and prayer. Others see Christ inviting them to come and join him in the deep.

Across these weeks in Lent we have been descending with the "Christ of the Deep." As we repeatedly have looked at the second chapter of Philippians, we have been following the words of what was probably an ancient hymn that the apostle Paul plucked out of the worship life of the early church. It begins in the highest reaches of divine glory with the One who was equal with God. The writer of the Fourth Gospel calls him "the Word," the One who "was in the beginning with God"; the One through whom "all things came into being" (John 1:1-3).

But Paul declares that the One who was equal with God did not see equality with God as something to be clutched or held tightly. Instead, he emptied himself, "poured himself out." He divested himself of his divine prerogatives, descended into this world as a humble servant, and settled down among us in our human flesh. It is the fulfillment of John's affirmation that "the Word became flesh and lived among us" (John 1:14). It was the ultimate expression of the angelic promise that his name would be Emmanuel, which means "God is with us" (Matthew 1:23).

Along the way of that plummeting descent from the heights of his divinity to the depths of our humanity, the question lurking in the background of the story is this: How far will he go? How far will this One who was equal with God descend to be one with us? How deeply will he dive into the real stuff of our ordinary, human existence?

The story the church proclaims during Holy Week provides the earthshaking, soul-shaping answer. He was "obedient to the point of death— / even death on a cross" (Philippians 2:8). There was no stopping along the way, no short-circuiting of the process, no detour, no easy escape. The One of whom this hymn sings did not just skim across the surface of our human life. He is the "Christ of the Deep" who descended into the deepest places of human suffering and pain. He is "God with us" in the darkest depths of our willful rebellion against the will and way of God. He is the "Christ of the Abyss" who descends with us into the dark abyss of death. He is God with us, even to death, even death on the cross.

The gospel lesson takes us to a critical turning point along the way of Christ's descent, into the garden where, shortly before his betrayal, arrest, and crucifixion, Jesus prayed, "Father, if you are willing, remove this cup from me; yet, not my will but yours be done" (Luke 22:42; see Luke 22:39-46). Make no mistake about it: For Jesus, this was a moment of genuine personal choice. He had to decide how far he would go in obedience to the redemptive love and saving purpose of God. He could choose either to be obedient to the way of self-emptying love, even if it meant going to the cross, or to look for some subtle compromise with the way of self-interest and self-protection.

And in that hour, Jesus chose what Dietrich Bonhoeffer called "single-minded obedience" to the way of self-giving love, even if it meant going to the cross.

The story would be powerful enough if we could find a way to hold it at arm's length, to keep it in the past, even to honor or adore it, but to keep it at a great distance from the real stuff of our daily lives. But the apostle will not let us have it that way. Paul tells us that this is not just a onetime event that happened in the life of Jesus in the past; it is intended to be the continuing pattern of life for Jesus' followers in the present.

We began this Lenten journey by saying that the apostle is out to change our minds. We've been discovering that the Christian life is not about a tidy rearrangement of the surface stuff of life but that it moves down into the deepest part of our being. It is about a radical reorientation in the way we think that results in a radical reorientation in the way we live. Paul calls for nothing short of a mental transplant in which the same mind-set with which Jesus came, lived, died, and rose again becomes the mind-set in which we live our lives, face our deaths, and hope for resurrection.

We've been catching a glimpse of what it might look like to live with the mind-set of Christ.

It is a mind-set of *love*—and not just any kind of love, but specifically the self-giving, self-emptying love of God revealed in Christ.

It is a mind-set of *servanthood*—a way of living that breaks our addiction to the "me-first mind-set" of the culture around us and teaches us that we are not here to be served but to serve.

It is a mind-set of *faithful* suffering—a way of sharing in the suffering of Christ for the world.

It is a mind-set of *surrender*—a way of living that calls us to let go of our own prerogatives and to learn to deny ourselves, take up our cross daily, and follow him.

It is a mind-set of *humility*—a way of living in which we learn not to take ourselves too seriously and to treat every other person as if he or she were the guest of honor at the table.

And now, as we move into the drama of Holy Week, the question turns on us. The question is no longer, How far will *he* go? The question becomes, How far will *you* go? How far will you go in allowing the mind-set of Jesus to become the mind-set by which you live? What practical, life-altering step of obedience are you willing to take in order to have the same mind, be of the same love, live with the same attitude as Jesus? How far will we go in following Jesus in the way that led to the cross?

When he was the Dean of the Chapel at Duke University, William H. Willimon asked some tough questions about newspaper advertising for the chapel. "What," he asked, "are we to say? *Are you happy, content, well situated? Come to the Chapel this Sunday and Jesus will relieve you of all that! . . . What are you doing this Sunday at eleven? Would you like to be crucified?*" Willimon went on to confess, "When you think about some of the stuff Jesus said . . . it's a wonder to me that any of you are here on a Sunday" (Michael A. Turner and William F. Malambri III, eds., *A Peculiar Prophet* [Nashville: Abingdon Press, 2004], 79-80, italics Willimon's).

Sooner or later, every follower of Jesus will come to his or her own Garden of Gethsemane, to places where we must choose to follow the way of self-giving love or the way of self-centered addiction, the way of generosity or the way of greed, the way of humility or the way of arrogant pride, the way of servanthood or the way of self-interest, the way of surrender or the way of control, the way of death that leads to life, or a way of life that ultimately leads to death. We come to the cross in the ordinary patterns of our lives, in those times and places where we decide to follow Jesus even if it means denying ourselves, taking up a cross, and following him.

On Palm Sunday in our church, we invited people to come to the Communion rail and pick up a small wooden cross on a braided string to hang around their necks. We made it clear that the crosses were not for everyone. They were for anyone who was ready to take some new, specific, concrete step of obedience to the way of Christ in his or her life. We believed that for some people, picking up one of those crosses would be a momentous decision that would mark the beginning of their life of discipleship. For others, it would bear witness to a significant change of mind-set, a different way of thinking, living, or acting. And for others, it would mark a small seemingly insignificant choice that reflected their next step in a growing life of obedience to Christ.

I was moved, though not surprised, as I watched people come down the aisle, kneel at the Communion rail, and take up a cross. What surprised me was later during the week when I met people around the city and saw that small wooden cross hanging around their necks. One man told me that he had never worn anything like that before and that this was his first public witness to his Christian faith. Another told me that he wore it under his shirt. Every time he felt it rub across his chest, he was reminded of the obedience of Christ. One woman described the way one of her coworkers saw the cross and asked for prayer. For each of them, picking up the cross marked a change in their way of thinking that resulted in a change in the way they lived their lives.

We are invited to follow the "Christ of the Abyss," the One who goes all the way down into the depths of human experience, the One who went to the cross, the One who calls us to follow.

Questions for Discussion and Reflection

1. The statue of *Christ of the Deep* serves as a powerful image of Christ for people who have seen it. What images of Christ speak to you in a powerful, compelling way, and how? What images of Christ have you seen that reflect his obedience to God's will and his servanthood? If possible, use your local library or the Internet to locate an image of the underwater *Christ of the Deep* statue located in the Florida Keys or the original *Christ of the Abyss* statue located in the Mediterranean Sea. How does this image speak to you? How does it capture the movement of the text from Philippians 2:6-11?

2. Review the themes we have studied thus far during this Lenten journey: love, servanthood, faithful suffering, surrender, humility, and obedience. Which of these themes make the most sense to you or seem the most compelling? How has each of them changed the way you think about the Christian life? Which one has been the most problematic for you, and why?

3. How will you prepare for Holy Week this year? What will you do to allow the passion story—the story of Christ's living among us, his suffering, and his death—to become reality in your life?

4. When have you experienced "Gethsemane"—a place where you had to choose between following "the way of self-giving love or the way of self-centered addiction, the way of generosity or the way of greed, the way of humility or the way of arrogant pride, the way of servanthood or the way of self-interest, the way of surrender or the way of control, the way of death that leads to life, or a way of life that ultimately leads to death?" How have you faced a decision that involved obedience to the way of Christ?

5. Have you ever worn a cross? If so, what did it mean to you? What importance do outward symbols of your faith have? Explain your answer as fully as possible.

Prayer

Endless scenes of wonder rise
With that mysterious tree,
Crucified before our eyes
Where we our Maker see:
Jesus, Lord, what Hast thou done?
Publish we the death Divine,
Stop, and gaze, and fall, and own
Was never love like thine!

> (*John and Charles Wesley: Selected Prayers, Hymns, Journal Notes, Sermons, Letters and Treatises*, Frank Whaling, ed. [New York: Paulist Press, 1981], 252)

Focus for the Week

The Christ of the Deep invites us to follow him to the cross.

Glory: Unexpected Glory!

Luke 24:1-12; Philippians 2:1-11

A fellow pastor told the delightful story of a little girl in his congregation who was almost as excited about Easter as she had been on Christmas Eve. Her father, wanting to be sure that she had some sense of what Easter meant, asked, "Nicole, do you know what Easter means?" She replied, "Yes." Her father asked, "Well, what does Easter mean?" A huge smile spread across the little girl's face. She raised her arms in the air and shouted at the top of her lungs, "Surprise!"

There is a little child inside of me who wants to respond the way Nicole did. As the sun rises on Easter morning, I'd like to throw my arms up in the air, lean back, look up into the sky, and shout, "Surprise!" Some year, I may even begin the Easter worship service by doing it!

The Gospel writers would say that Nicole got it right. Each Gospel writer tells the resurrection story differently. The incoherence of the disciples' reports from the empty tomb bears witness to the way the whole experience simply blew them away. Their words and stories tumble out of their doubt and joy. The one thing they all have in common is that their experience of the risen Christ came as a surprise. Not one of them expected it. The shock took their breath away and left them stuttering and stumbling in confusion.

There were hints of the possibility of resurrection in the Old Testament, to be sure. And in the New Testament, Jesus predicted it at least three times (see Matthew 16:21; 17:22-23; 20:17-19). But most of the people around Jesus at the time, including the disciples, had very little, if any, expectation that resurrection would actually happen.

Luke's account focuses on the women who had followed Jesus from Galilee, all the way to the cross. When they could no longer follow Jesus, Luke says, they followed Joseph of Arimathea, who carried Jesus' body to the tomb (see Luke 23:50-56).

My favorite place in our nation's capital is the Washington National Cathedral. My favorite spot in the Cathedral is the Chapel of Saint Joseph of Arimathea. It's in the basement, directly beneath the crossing, the place where the length of the nave crosses the north and south transepts and leads to the chancel, forming the building in the shape of a cross. The chapel walls are defined by the huge, rounded stone pillars that provide the foundation for the tower that soars up into the clouds, providing the highest vantage point in the District of Columbia. (You might try viewing the chapel at www.cathedral.org/cathedral/discover/joseph.shtml.)

The focal point of Saint Joseph's Chapel is a magnificent painting of the burial of Jesus. Jan Henrik DeRosen used Cathedral choristers and employees as models for his painting of Joseph leading the procession to the tomb. Jesus' mother is there, supported by the apostle John. A nameless young man who helps bear the lifeless body on his shoulder looks directly into the congregation, drawing us into the cold grief of the mourners. By all human expectations, this was the end of the story. Death had closed the door on the life and ministry of Jesus.

Luke says that the women followed Joseph of Arimathea and watched as he laid the lifeless body of Jesus in the tomb. Then, because it was the Sabbath, they returned to their homes to prepare the spices they would need for embalming. These women were solid realists. They were prepared to deal with death.

There is a sense in which we all are a lot like those women. Sooner or later, we are the ones who are left to manage the final arrangements for a loved one or friend. We know what needs to be done. There are people to call, a service to plan, flowers to order, a final resting place to be chosen. The congregation I serve has even provided a workbook on end-of-life planning for the members of our congregation. We know what to do with death.

Then, early in the morning on the first day of the week, the women headed off toward the tomb with the spices they had prepared. Embalming Jesus' mangled body would be gruesome, ugly work, but they were prepared for it. As they came to the tomb that morning, the only thing they expected was the dark stench of death.

Then, the unexpected happened: When they got to the tomb, they found the stone that covered the entrance rolled away! The body was gone! The tomb was empty! In the place of death, they heard the most unexpected question that had ever been asked in the long history of this death-addicted planet: "Why do you seek the living among the dead?" (Luke 24:5 RSV). It's no wonder that Luke says the women were perplexed! Why wouldn't they be? Then they heard the most surprising announcement ever spoken: "He is not here. He is risen!" (Luke 24:5*b*, paraphrased).

Craig Barnes, when he was pastor of the National Presbyterian Church in Washington, said, "Easter is the last thing we are expecting. . . . It's about more hope than we can handle" ("Savior at Large," *The Christian Century*, March 13-20, 2002, p. 16). The only way to hear the Easter story is to listen for the gasp of surprise that took the followers' breath away, to feel the jolt that sent their heartbeats racing, and to stand frozen in awestricken amazement at the surprising way God broke into the dark predictability of death and brought to life something they never expected.

The truth about your life and mine is that, far too often, we don't expect resurrection either. Conditioned by the mind-set of the world around us, we expect dead things to stay dead. We expect the past to stay in the past. We expect broken hearts to stay broken. We expect might to make right and violence somehow to bring peace. We expect this sin-twisted, violence-addicted, greed-infested world to go on pretty much the same way it always has.

We don't expect broken relationships to be healed. We don't expect shattered hopes to be restored. We don't expect swords to be turned into plowshares and spears into pruning hooks. We don't expect the sick to be healed, the hungry to be fed, the lame to walk, the blind to see, the lost to be found, and the prisoners to be set free. We don't expect to find new life in the place of death.

Like the women on the way to the tomb, we live with a mind-set that is prepared to deal with death, darkness, hostility, and fear. But we are just as perplexed as they were when it comes to dealing with life. When the glory of God intersects with our human experience, it always takes us by surprise and blows our minds.

And so, the apostle challenges us one more time to have the same mind in us that was in Christ Jesus. The Easter gospel calls for nothing less than a mental transplant in which the same mind-set with which Jesus lived, died, and rose again becomes the mind-set by which we live, face our death, and hope for resurrection.

When we read the ancient hymn of the descending Christ (see Philippians 2:5-11), did you notice the shift in the subject of the verbs? In describing the way of self-emptying obedience, Christ is the subject of the active verb. He "emptied himself." He "humbled himself." He took the form of a servant. He "became obedient to the point of death" (see vv. 7 and 8). That's his part, and that's our part in the process as well. We, like Jesus, are called to active obedience to the way and will of God's self-giving love.

But at the word *therefore* (v. 9), the sentence structure changes. God becomes the subject of the active verb. "Therefore," because of Christ's self-emptying obedience, "God also highly exalted him / and gave him the name / that is above every name" (Philippians 2:9).

The verbs make the action clear. Our part is active obedience all the way to death. God's part is resurrection. The new life of the resurrection is not something we make, create, manipulate, or control. It is not something we carry within us. It is the direct action of God, who alone can bring unexpected life and hope out of the predictable darkness of fear and death.

Paul forces the choice upon us: Which mind-set, attitude, or perspective will we choose? Will we live with the predictable mind-set of the death-addicted world? Or will we choose to live with the mind-set of the risen Christ? Will we continue to live within the narrow, predictable boundaries of the world around us? Or will we choose to live within the unexpected, unpredictable, life-giving power of a risen Christ?

Dr. William Sloane Coffin Jr., while he was the senior minister at the Riverside Church in New York City, preached one of the best Easter sermons I've heard. Dr. Coffin acknowledged that we are often tempted to believe that we live in a "Good Friday world." My own definition of a "Good Friday world" is one where the crowd continues to choose the release of Barabbas rather than Jesus, and where Pilate continues to wash his hands of responsibility; where peace continues to be scourged by violence; where love still gets nailed to the cross by hate; where life gets buried in the dark tomb of death.

But Dr. Coffin said that the resurrection means that, in spite of all appearances to the contrary, this is an Easter world after all. Christ is risen—present tense—and one day the whole created order will bend its knee and recognize him as Lord. Here are Dr. Coffin's words:

> By all appearances, it is a Good Friday world. But by the light of Easter . . . we can dimly discern a "Yes, but" kind of message. Yes, fear and self-righteousness, indifference and sentimentality kill; but love never dies, not with God, and not even with us. . . . Christ is risen *pro nobis*, for us, to put love in our hearts, decent thoughts in our heads, and a little more iron up our spines. Christ is risen to convert us, not from life to something more than life, but from something less than life to the possibility of full life itself.

William Sloane Coffin concluded his sermon with this penetrating question: "Are we going to continue the illusion of a Good Friday world, or start living the reality of an Easter one?" (William Sloane Coffin, *Living the Truth in a World of Illusions* [San Francisco: Harper & Row, 1985], 70, 74). In other words, will we choose to live with the predictable mind-set of the world around us, or will we choose to live with the mind-set of the risen Christ? Will we face life in fear of death, or will we face death in the hope of new life?

I remember the summer we spent our vacation in my little hometown in western Pennsylvania, walking along the tree-lined streets between my mother's home and the local hospital where we were waiting for my paternal grandfather to die. He was unconscious when we arrived, but he hung on for more than a week. One of the nurses said, "The city doctors who come up here from Pittsburgh are always surprised by how strong these old coal miners are." Day after day, members of the family stood beside his bed as the signs on the monitors slowly declined. I was there with my Uncle Frank when the lines finally went flat and he was gone.

That spring I had heard Beethoven's Mass in C for the first time. Beethoven's setting of the Nicene Creed blew my mind. I've never gotten over it. I'm convinced that when the angel choirs in heaven affirm the creed, they sing it the way Beethoven set it to music. In English, the modern version of the creed ends with the affirmation that "we look for the resurrection of the dead, and the life of the world to come." But in Latin, the words are *"et expecto resurrectionem mortuorum."* Beethoven has the choir repeat the phrase *"et expecto,"* louder and stronger each time, reinforcing that we do not merely *believe* in the resurrection as an intellectual concept; we *expect* it!

More than a decade has passed since the summer my grandfather died, but I've never forgotten the way the *"et expecto"* of the creed reverberated in my memory as I watched his last, labored breaths. Eight summers earlier, we had buried my father in the same hillside cemetery to which we would carry my grandfather's body. From a human standpoint, that's all we could expect. It was the end of their stories. Death is the one absolutely predictable reality for every one of us. But to affirm the creed is to expect more than death. By faith in Christ, we face death in the sure expectation of the "resurrection of the dead, and the life of the world to come." We live with the expectation that, when our story is over, the God who raised Jesus from the dead will raise us as well. Even more, we expect that the resurrection is not just for individual human beings but that God promises to save and restore this whole broken and dying creation. In the resurrection, nothing will be left behind.

Early in my ministry, I learned the difference an Easter mind-set makes from a woman I met when I was invited to preach at a church in Georgia. As soon as I arrived, the pastor took me to visit her. I think she needed to check out the visiting preacher to make sure he was fit to be in her church. She had been suffering from a vicious form of brain cancer for nearly five years. Her frail body bore the evidence of the surgeries, the treatments, and the devastating effects of the disease. There was no question that her death was near. But her eyes were strong and clear, and her face was filled with gentleness and peace. As we were concluding our visit, I asked her the question I've often asked people in her condition: "What have you learned?" And I'll confess that I was not prepared for her response. It took me by surprise. I was prepared to hear her say something about the love of her family, the support and encouragement of her congregation, or perhaps her hope for life beyond death. But I never expected the smile that spread across her face. She looked me straight in the eye, and with more conviction than I expected, she said, "Oh, just one thing: Jesus is Lord!" She faced death with an Easter mind-set that was something like the mind-set with which Jesus had faced the cross.

The early hymn or affirmation that Paul pasted into his letter to the Philippians concludes with a resounding note of confident praise: "Therefore God also highly exalted him / and gave him the name / that is above every name, / so that at the name of Jesus / every knee should bend, / . . . and every tongue confess that Jesus Christ is Lord, / to the glory of God the Father" (Philippians 2:9-11). And the best surprise of all is that the risen Christ can be your Lord, too!

Questions for Discussion and Reflection

1. What do you feel on Easter Sunday morning? How have you experienced the surprise of the resurrection?

2. How have you learned to deal with death? When have you "walked with the women" to lay to rest someone you loved? What do you feel when you read the story of the burial of Jesus?

3. Do you agree that "conditioned by the mind-set of the world around us, we expect dead things to stay dead"? Why or why not?

4. Reread Philippians 2:5-11 and take notice how the subject of the active verbs changes—from *Christ Jesus* in verses 6 through 8, to *God,* beginning with verse 9. What does that change mean to you?

5. How does the message of William Sloane Coffin's Easter sermon speak to you? When have you felt that you were living in a "Good Friday world"? When have you experienced an "Easter world"?

6. As we conclude our Lenten journey, how has your mind changed? What new insights have you received? What practical difference will they make in your life?

Prayer

Almighty God, who through your only-begotten Son Jesus Christ overcame death and opened to us the gate of everlasting life: Grant that we, who celebrate with joy the day of the Lord's resurrection, may be raised from the death of sin by your life-giving Spirit; through Jesus Christ our Lord, who lives and reigns with you and the Holy Spirit, one God, now and for ever. Amen (*Book of Common Prayer* [New York: Seabury Press, 1979], 222).

Focus for the Week

The new life of the resurrection is not something we make, create, manipulate, or control. It is the direct action of the God who surprises us by bringing unexpected life and hope out of the predictable darkness of fear and death.